THE MYSTERY OF
Darwin's Frog

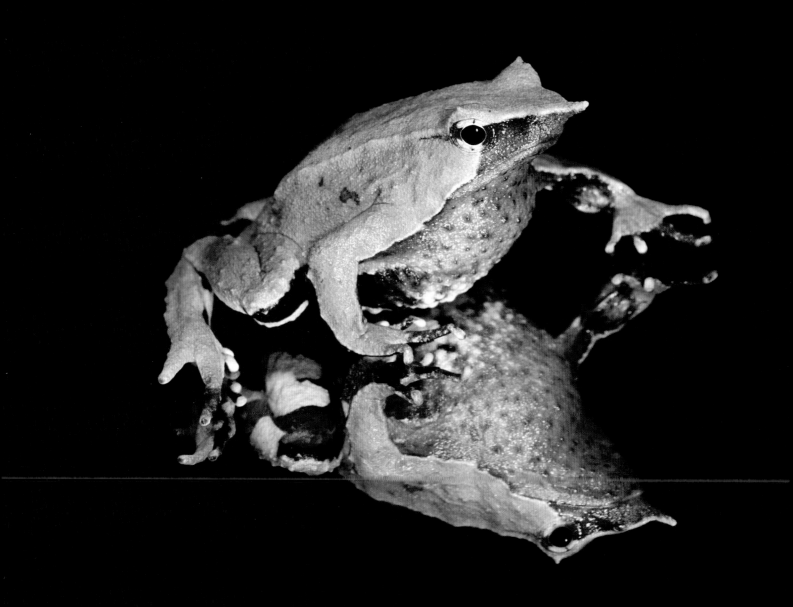

THE MYSTERY OF
Darwin's Frog

MARTY CRUMP

Illustrations by **STEVE JENKINS** and **EDEL RODRIGUEZ**

BOYDS MILLS PRESS
AN IMPRINT OF HIGHLIGHTS
Honesdale, Pennsylvania

This is a story of discovery: how we know what we know about Darwin's frogs. The story combines history and biology and involves an international cast of characters. Scientists are still solving mysteries and writing new chapters in this story of one of the world's most unusual frogs.

a n emerald-green frog sits on wet moss. As he opens his mouth wide, out hops a tiny gray frog no bigger than your smallest fingernail. It leaps, tumbles, and stubs its nose as it lands.

What just happened is part of the amazing story of Darwin's frogs. As you'll see, scientists are still unraveling mysteries surrounding these unusual animals.

Darwin's frogs live on the ground in this forest in southern Chile, often near slowly running streams or in swampy areas.

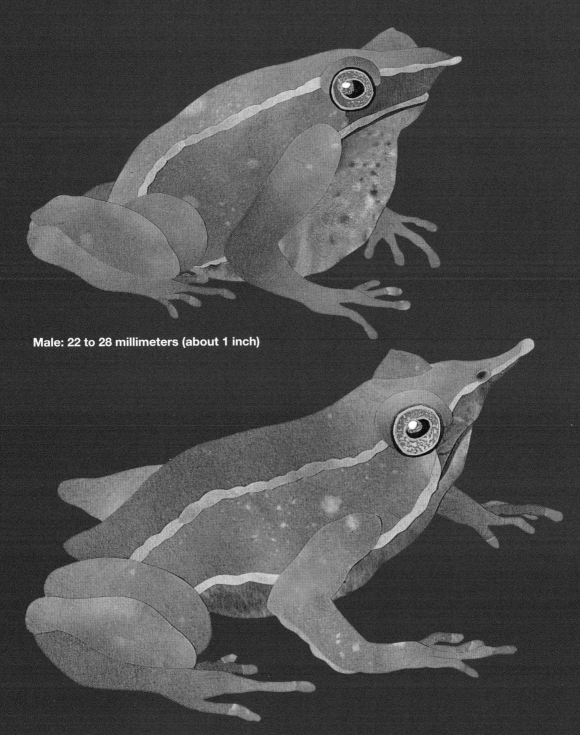

Male: 22 to 28 millimeters (about 1 inch)

Female: Up to 31 millimeters (1.2 inches)

Where Do Darwin's Frogs Live?
During his now-famous voyage on the ship HMS *Beagle* from 1831 to 1836, Charles Darwin found some of the frogs later named after him in a forest near Valdivia, Chile. Darwin's frogs (*ranitas de Darwin* in Spanish) live only in central to southern Chile and in south-central Argentina, near the border with Chile. They live from sea level up to 1,500 meters (4,921 feet) in the mountains.

The story of their discovery began more than 175 years ago with a British naturalist named Charles Darwin. Darwin is famous for his ideas about evolution. When he was twenty-two years old, he joined a scientific expedition around the world. His job was to be a gentleman companion to the ship's captain. He was also the naturalist on board. To find out what plants and animals lived where, Darwin collected and preserved specimens, which he sent back to England.

In December 1834, while on the island of Lemuy in southern Chile, Darwin found an unusual frog with a flap of skin on its nose. Then, in February 1835, while exploring what he called a "thick & gloomy forest" near Valdivia, Chile, Darwin found more of the same pointy-nosed little frogs. In his journal, Darwin described these frogs as "very pretty & curious." He had never seen such frogs anywhere.

Charles Darwin

Darwin's frogs can be green, cream, brown, rusty red, or a combination of these colors. Their throats and chests are chestnut brown, and their bellies are marbled jet black and snow white.

Scientists from far and wide marveled over Darwin's preserved specimens housed in European museums. The treasures from his journey ranged from beetles to foxes. He had found many new species—every naturalist's dream!

No one could identify Darwin's pointy-nosed frog. It was clearly a new species. In 1841, two French scientists—André Marie Constant Duméril and Gabriel Bibron—named this little frog *Rhinoderma darwinii*. *Rhinoderma* means "nose skin" in Greek. The second part, *darwinii*, honors the frog's discoverer.

In 1848, a French zoologist, Antoine Guichenot, examined Darwin's specimens. Imagine his surprise when he discovered tadpoles inside one of the frogs. Guichenot assumed that the frog was a female and that Darwin's frogs give birth to live young.

That idea was intriguing. Very few frogs give birth to live young. Most frogs lay eggs. As exciting as the idea was, it was wrong.

In Paris during the early to mid-1800s, André Marie Constant Duméril and his main assistant, Gabriel Bibron, studied animals that had been collected from around the world. The two published the first technical descriptions of hundreds of new species of amphibians and reptiles, giving a scientific name to each species, including *Rhinoderma darwinii*, the Darwin's frog.

Gabriel Bibron

André Marie Constant Duméril

The flap of skin on the nose of Darwin's frogs varies in length. Some frogs have short stubs. Others, like this one, have longer flaps.

The inflated vocal sac of a male frog, in this case a toad, broadcasts the sound of its call to nearby individuals.

In 1872, Spanish zoologist Marcos Jiménez de la Espada examined other specimens of Darwin's frogs from Valdivia. Instead of finding tadpoles inside of females, he found tadpoles inside of five males. How did he know? The frogs had vocal sacs—throat pouches that fill with air when males call. Females do not have vocal sacs.

How could males have tadpoles inside their bodies? Had they eaten the tadpoles? No. Jiménez de la Espada wrote that "without a shadow of doubt," the tadpoles were inside the vocal sacs.

But how had they gotten there?

The explanation remained a mystery for another sixty years. During that time, scientists who studied frogs mostly caught, described, and named the animals.

By the 1930s, scientists became more interested in the behavior of animals. One of those scientists, Ottmar Wilhelm, from the University of Concepción in Chile, decided to focus on the behavior of Darwin's frogs. Hoping to see how the tadpoles ended up in the male's vocal sac, Wilhelm put some of the frogs in terraria. One day a female laid eggs in the moss, and a male fertilized them. Every day, Wilhelm watched the new parents. The mother frog ignored her eggs. But the father frog stayed near them. Occasionally, he ate an insect walking by. Several weeks later, the tadpoles wriggled, squirmed, turned somersaults inside their jelly capsules, and then hatched. Wilhelm watched the male slurp the tadpoles into his mouth.

Bingo! That explained how tadpoles end up in their fathers' vocal sacs.

Marcos Jiménez de la Espada

Taking a photograph of a male Darwin's frog slurping up his eggs or tadpoles is extremely hard to do. The frog does the job quickly—and secretively. This illustration is based on a drawing made by biologist Klaus Busse from his video recordings of the frogs in action.

A male Darwin's frog watches over his eggs. Females lay up to fifteen eggs in a clutch. The eggs are about 3.6 millimeters wide (0.14 inch)—more than twice the size of most other frog eggs.

Eggs

Male Darwin's frogs either slurp the eggs into their mouths just before they hatch, or they gobble up the tadpoles right after they hatch.

These tiny baby Darwin's frogs have just hopped out of their father's mouth. About 90 percent of all frog species abandon their young. In most of the other 10 percent, the female takes care of the young. In only a few species, such as Darwin's frogs, it's the male.

Froglets

The tadpoles grow and develop inside their fathers for about two months. Eventually, tiny frogs crawl from the vocal sac into their father's mouth. He opens wide, and the babies hop out. No other frog "burps up" its young.

But tadpoles need food to develop into frogs. What do they eat inside their father's vocal sac?

Tadpoles of Darwin's frogs hatch with large amounts of yolk. For a while they get food by absorbing this yolk into their bodies. But this may be only part of their nourishment.

In the 1970s, three scientists from Valdivia, Chile, studied the vocal sacs of Darwin's frogs. Oscar Goicoechea, Orlando Garrido, and Boris Jorquera found signs that the inside lining of the vocal sac releases substances. They wondered: Do tadpoles "eat" these substances?

The scientists carried out an experiment to answer this question. Based on their results, it seems likely that substances released from the vocal sac pass through the skin of young tadpoles and into the intestine of older ones.

Is that how tadpoles get enough nourishment to develop into frogs? If so, Darwin's frogs are the only frogs in which males "feed" their tadpoles.

The vocal sac of a male Darwin's frog becomes greatly enlarged when he broods (carries) his tadpoles. During this time, he does not call, but he does eat.

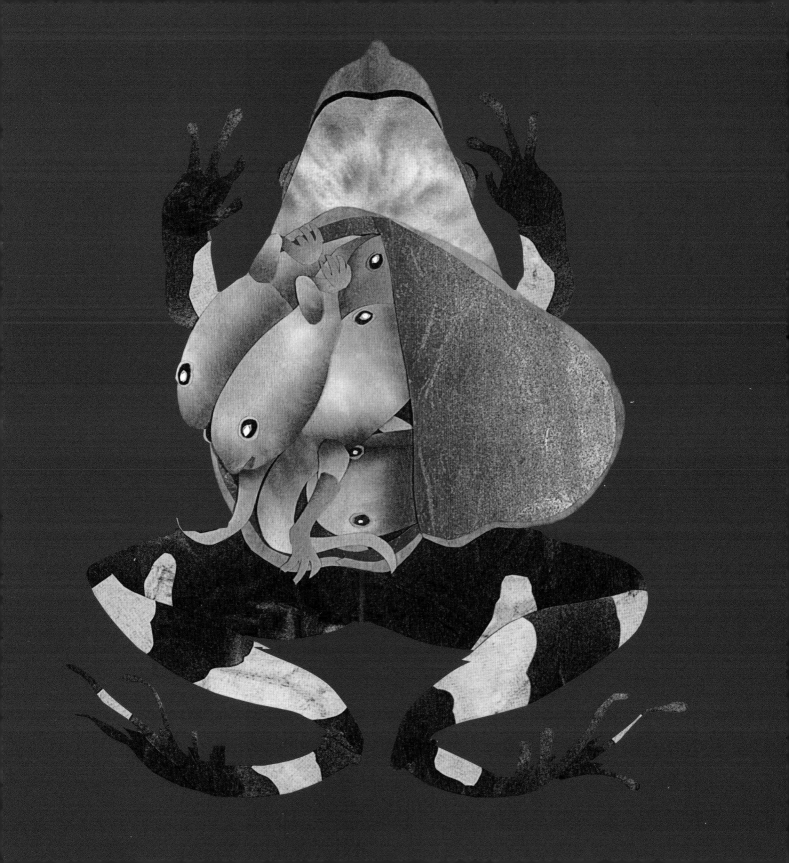

The next part of the story is an example of serendipity—making discoveries by chance. When he was a student in Chile, Klaus Busse studied how gray wood frogs reproduce. Later, in Germany, he studied birds. After that, he started working with fish at the Museum Koenig in Bonn, Germany. His research has come full circle, and he is now the world's expert on Darwin's frogs.

As a child, Busse spent summers with his cousins near Valdivia, Chile, where they explored a nearby forest he once described as "magical." Busse was especially enchanted with the little pointy-nosed Darwin's frogs.

In the 1980s, when he returned to Germany after a trip to Chile, he took some Darwin's frogs with him. He thought, *They will remind me of my "magical" forest, the smell of wet trees, and the raindrops on my face.*

Back at the museum, Busse set up the frogs in outdoor terraria. These frog apartments provided hiding places for the frogs and running water that flowed over moss.

Busse spent many hours watching the frogs. He wondered what he would learn. His work required patience. He hesitated to leave the terraria even for a minute, for fear of missing something. Thanks to his patience, Busse often observed the frogs' courtship behavior.

Courtship starts when a male calls *peeep, peeep, peeep,* like a baby duck. If a female is ready to lay her eggs, she hops toward the male. Then the frogs do something unusual.

Klaus Busse

Klaus Busse's terraria for watching frogs are kept outdoors at the Museum Koenig in Bonn, Germany.

These Darwin's frogs are almost ready to lay and fertilize eggs. The female is the green-and-brown frog.

They engage in what Busse calls "jump-onto-kick-off" behavior. *Bam*! The male bumps into the female. *Wham*! She kicks him with her back legs. He loses his balance, tumbles away, picks himself up, and crashes into her again. *Bam*! She delivers another powerful kick.

When Busse first saw this behavior he gasped, "Are the frogs crazy? Am I crazy? Frogs don't do this!"

The next day, Busse sat in front of the terrarium with his video camera. The frogs bumped, kicked, and tumbled. He now had proof that he wasn't imagining the odd behavior.

Busse thinks the female might use this behavior to choose a mate. Males must be strong to brood tadpoles for two months. Perhaps a female can gauge a male's stamina by how far he tumbles when she kicks him. If he tumbles too far, he might be weak, and he might not make such a good father. If he moves only a little, he might be strong and a terrific protector.

If the female is satisfied with how a male reacts, she follows him into his hiding place. She lays her eggs under a piece of wood or stone. Her babies' fates will soon be in her mate's hands . . . er, vocal sac.

After the female lays her eggs, ten to eleven weeks pass before the baby frogs emerge from the father's mouth.

These illustrations are based on drawings made by biologist Klaus Busse from his video recordings of Darwin's frogs in action.

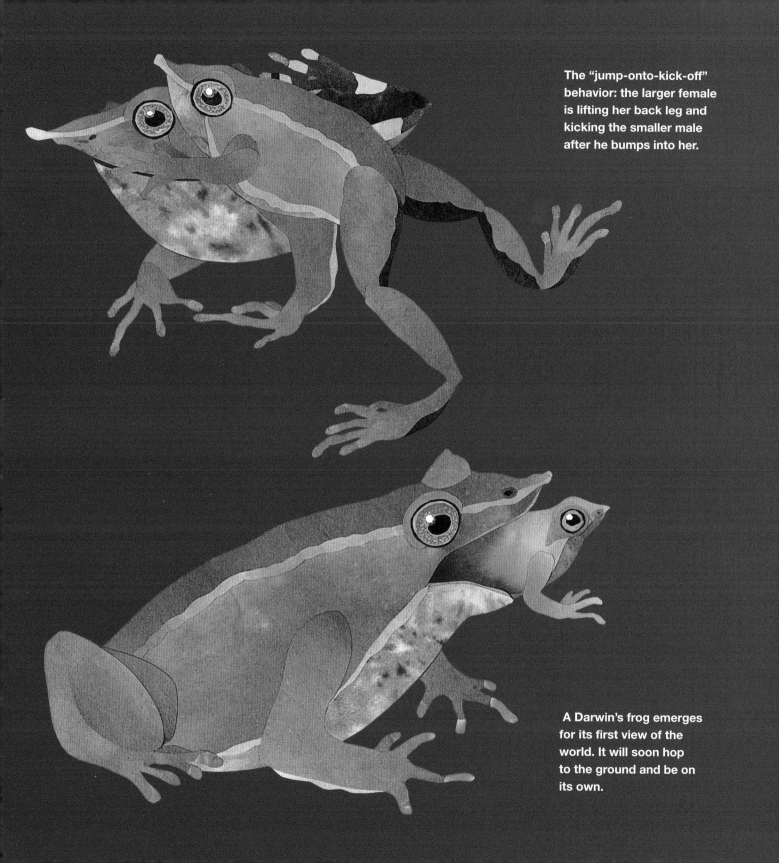

The "jump-onto-kick-off" behavior: the larger female is lifting her back leg and kicking the smaller male after he bumps into her.

A Darwin's frog emerges for its first view of the world. It will soon hop to the ground and be on its own.

Melimoyu, home to many Darwin's frogs, is almost as far south as the frogs live.

In the 1990s, I too became involved in the story of Darwin's frog. I had read about the frogs years before when I was a young herpetologist, and I could hardly believe their story. Over the years, I studied many frogs in Costa Rica, Brazil, Ecuador, and Argentina. Finally, in 1994 I visited Chile and fulfilled my dream of seeing Darwin's frogs.

I realized that scientists still didn't know much about how Darwin's frogs live in the wild. I decided to visit the frogs' native habitat to learn what I could. Lauren, my seventeen-year-old niece, volunteered to be my field assistant. In November 1999, we traveled almost to the bottom of the world, to Melimoyu in southern Chile.

At the time, Melimoyu was an isolated fishing village with twenty-five people and hundreds of Darwin's frogs. Lauren and I stayed with a family in a small wooden cottage for more than two weeks. The cottage had no electricity, indoor toilets, or beds, but we ate like queens—freshly caught fish and clams, and bread baked in a wood stove.

Our first day in Melimoyu, on one of our explorations, Lauren giggled. "Aunt Marty, I just found the Pillsbury Doughboy!" It was the chubbiest roly-poly brooding male I had ever seen.

I was curious about the behavior of brooding males. I figured they would make especially good meals for predators— adult frogs with tadpole centers. I wondered: Do brooding males hide to avoid being eaten? Do they hang out in different places than females and nonbrooding males do?

Left: Sunrise near Melimoyu
Below: A male Darwin's frog
with his vocal sac full of young

Every day, Lauren and I bundled up in long underwear, down jackets, and heavy-duty rain gear to watch frogs. We struggled to keep warm and dry.

Since warmer temperatures allow tadpoles to develop faster, I wondered if brooding males sought warmer areas to brood. Using a digital thermometer, we measured the temperature of the exact spot where we found each frog—on the surface of dirt, fallen leaves, or moss. We found that, compared to other adults, brooding males hung out in warmer areas. Just as you get warmer in direct sunlight, brooding males heat their bodies in warm spots, and their tadpoles can develop faster.

We thought the brooding males might become less active to avoid being eaten. Maybe they would hide. So we also recorded the activities of frogs during twenty-minute blocks of time. Lauren and I found that brooding males were just as active as nonbrooding males and females. Despite their precious cargo, brooding males still needed to search for their insect dinners.

So how do Darwin's frogs protect themselves from predators?

Above left: Lauren watches a Darwin's frog through binoculars. To study the frogs' activity level, we observed each frog for twenty minutes and wrote down the number of times it hopped.

Above right: We marked the location of each Darwin's frog with flagging tape. Darwin's frogs stay in their "home" areas, so by marking the sites, we knew where to look for each frog.

Left: After measuring each Darwin's frog, we put it back in the exact place where we found it.

Who's Afraid of the Chucao?

In southern Chile, there is a superstition that if a chucao sings over your left shoulder, you should return home and quit work for the day. If you don't obey the warning, something bad might happen to you. There is a way to appease the chucao, though. Quickly say out loud: *"El canto para mí, las lombrices para ti"* ("The song for me, the worms for you"). The chucao will then allow you to continue safely on your way.

When Darwin's frogs sit still, they are hard to see. They are about the same size, color, and shape of southern beech tree leaves, which are often the most common tree in the frogs' habitat. In fact, a frog's pointed nose looks like a leaf petiole—the stalk that connects a leaf blade to the stem. A frog stays camouflaged by looking like a leaf on the ground.

But when they move, the frogs attract the attention of predators. For example, the frogs make tasty meals for the chucao (*chu-cow*), a brown bird with an orange chest and a black-and-white-striped belly. Chucaos hop along the forest floor. Like chickens, they scrape the ground with their feet, tossing dirt and leaves behind them as they search for food. If a frog happens to jump to avoid being crushed by a chucao's foot, the bird might grab the frog in its bill.

So what's a Darwin's frog to do? When disturbed, the frogs sometimes flip onto their backs and play dead. Because most predators don't eat dead frogs, a flipped-over frog has a better chance of surviving.

The chucao eats Darwin's frogs. The bird is about 16.5 centimeters (6.5 inches) long.

Darwin's frogs blend in with their environment. They look like these southern beech tree leaves that have fallen to the ground.

As I tried to photograph this Darwin's frog, it flipped over and played dead. Maybe it thought I was going to eat it.

23

Perhaps the biggest Darwin's-frog mystery so far in the twenty-first century is why the frogs are disappearing. Scientists wonder where the frogs still live and which places once had Darwin's frogs but now show no sign of them.

In some places, the frogs' disappearance is easy to understand. People have cut down native forest and planted pine and eucalyptus trees for lumber and firewood. Darwin's frogs cannot live in pine or eucalyptus plantations. The changes in moisture and ground cover, and new populations of insects now available for food, are not right for them.

But the frogs also have disappeared from protected habitats. What is the reason?

A part of the native forest was cut down to plant this stand of non-native eucalyptus trees in Chile.

Darwin's frog is only one of many species of frogs that are declining in protected areas in the world. Another is the golden toad (shown here), once found only in one mountain range of Costa Rica. The last golden toad was seen in 1989.

Like Darrwin's frog, the tree frog known as *Gastrotheca cornuta* is also declining in numbers.

A killer fungus is a likely possibility.

In the late 1990s, scientists discovered a fungus that attacks and kills some species of amphibians but not others. They named it *Batrachochytrium dendrobatidis*, or *Bd* for short. The fungus occurs in some areas but not in others. Has the fungus attacked Darwin's frogs? And if so, in which parts of the frog's range?

I am working with two other conservation biologists, Danté Fenolio and Andres Charrier, to answer these questions. So far we've surveyed twelve sites, from central to southern Chile. We search for frogs in moss and layers of fallen leaves. We wipe a sterile cotton swab over each frog's belly and legs. Then we put the swab in its own sterile container. Later, laboratory technicians examine the swabs to see if *Bd* is present.

The good news is that as of August 2012, *Bd* was present on frogs from only one of our study sites. But what happened to the Darwin's frogs that have disappeared from other protected sites? Could *Bd* have killed them?

The author swabs a frog for *Bd*.

Danté Fenolio, from the Atlanta Botanical Garden, cleaning his boots. After we leave a site, we soak our boots in bleach to kill any fungi that might be present. We do not want to carry the fatal *Bd* fungus from one place to another.

Andres Charrier, from the Pontifical Catholic University of Chile in Santiago, photographs a frog. We record all the species of frogs living with Darwin's frogs, and we swab individuals of these other species for the *Bd* fungus.

El Valle, a national park in the bowl of an inactive volcano in Panama, is home to the endangered golden frog.

Scientists know of no way to rid the environment of *Bd*. But we can move frogs to safety, with the hope that someday they, or their descendants, can go home.

Just such a rescue was performed in 2006. Scientists predicted that *Bd* would reach El Valle in Panama, Central America, soon thereafter. Many species of amphibians, including the endangered golden frog, lived there.

The scientists traveled to El Valle shortly before the fungus arrived. They collected six hundred frogs of thirty-five species and flew them back to Zoo Atlanta and the Atlanta Botanical Garden in Georgia. Many of these frogs are breeding in captivity. If El Valle becomes *Bd*-free in the future, descendants of the original frogs will be returned. *Bd* killed many frogs that remained in El Valle.

If the fungus begins to wipe out Darwin's frogs, a similar rescue could be attempted in Chile. The Atlanta Botanical Garden and the National Zoo of Chile have built a facility at the zoo to house rescued frogs if it comes to that point.

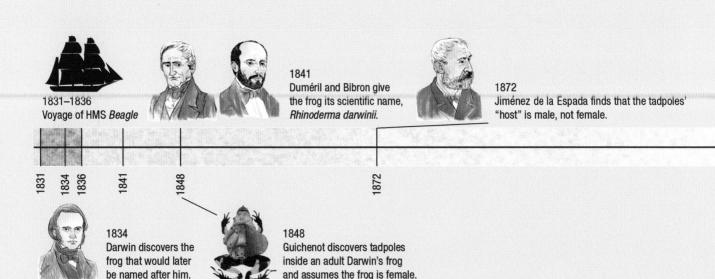

1831–1836
Voyage of HMS *Beagle*

1841
Duméril and Bibron give the frog its scientific name, *Rhinoderma darwinii*.

1872
Jiménez de la Espada finds that the tadpoles' "host" is male, not female.

1831 1834 1836 1841 1848 1872

1834
Darwin discovers the frog that would later be named after him.

1848
Guichenot discovers tadpoles inside an adult Darwin's frog and assumes the frog is female.

Golden frogs, found only in Panama, are critically endangered because of habitat destruction, specimen overcollecting, and exposure to *Bd*. Legend has it that anyone who finds one of these frogs will be rewarded with happiness and good luck. Let's hope that the frogs themselves will have the good fortune to survive.

1981
Busse begins behavioral studies using captive frogs.

1998
Pathogen that had been attacking frogs in Central America identified as a fungus. Fungus later named *Batrachochytrium dendrobatidis (Bd)*.

2002
Busse reports "jump-onto-kick-off" mating behavior.

2009
Major field research project led by Fenolio begins.

1932 · 1981 · 1986 · 1998 · 1999 · 2002 · 2006 · 2009 · 2010

1932
Wilhelm sees a male frog slurping up his tadpoles.

1986
Goicoechea, Garrido, and Jorquera find clues that the father may secrete nutrients from his vocal sac to feed his young.

1999
Crump observes brooding males seeking warm spots.

2006
Amphibians airlifted from fungus-contaminated forests in Panama.

2010
Amphibian facility completed.

For now, until the facility is needed to house rescued frogs, terraria there provide a home to healthy Darwin's frogs. After males start peeping, females lay eggs; then males brood tadpoles, and baby frogs hop out of their fathers' mouths.

If *Bd* wipes out Darwin's frogs in the wild, this captive population will serve as a safeguard against extinction. Another captive breeding program for Darwin's frogs has been established at the University of Concepción in Chile. All these efforts help give Darwin's frogs a better chance of surviving.

Probing the mystery of Darwin's frog has involved scientists from Europe, South America, and North America. These researchers have made their discoveries about Darwin's frogs using various methods. These include examination and dissection of preserved specimens, captive breeding, laboratory experiments, field observations, and analysis of skin swabs.

The story of the survival of Darwin's frogs begins a new chapter. The answer to one question sparks many new questions. That is how science works.

Meanwhile, back in the Chilean forest, male Darwin's frogs continue to burp up tiny babies. The babies wriggle into the wet moss, safe at the moment from chucaos, *Bd*, and people.

In parts of South America, you might hear, "*Viva ranitas de Darwin!*"—Long live Darwin's frogs!

Although scientists have learned much about Darwin's frogs, there are many more mysteries yet to be unraveled about these unique animals.

The amphibian facility at the National Zoo in Santiago, Chile, is prepared to house rescued frogs if *Bd* causes die-offs.

More about Darwin's Frogs

Darwin's Frog Tadpoles

Tadpoles of Darwin's frogs are different from most other tadpoles. Aquatic tadpoles have muscular tails bordered by delicate fins. Their strong tails allow the tadpoles to escape from predators quickly. *Rhinoderma darwinii* tadpoles, which don't swim in water, have small, weak tail fins. Most aquatic tadpoles scrape algae and bacteria from rocks and vegetation with rows of tiny "teeth." Tadpoles of Darwin's frogs do not have these projections.

How does a *Rhinoderma darwinii* tadpole breathe inside its father's vocal sac? This piece of the puzzle has not been answered yet. Scientists have an idea, though. Inside the vocal sac, foam made of air bubbles surrounds the tadpoles and may provide the needed oxygen.

Rhinoderma rufum—the Other *Rhinoderma*

In 1902, R. A. Philippi, director of the Museum of Natural History in Santiago, Chile, named a new frog species from central Chile—*Heminectes rufus*. For a long time, many scientists thought the species was the same as Darwin's frog. Finally, in 1975, scientists decided that *Heminectes rufus* was indeed different. What was distinctive about this frog?

These frogs lay twelve to twenty-five eggs in a clutch, instead of five to fifteen, as Darwin's frogs do. Their eggs are only two-thirds the size of *Rhinoderma darwinii* eggs. The eggs hatch after about seven days, instead of twenty. The fathers brood the tadpoles in their vocal sacs for about two weeks, instead of two months. Then the males hop to water and burp up the young while they are still tadpoles. After about three months of living in the water, the tadpoles metamorphose into tiny frogs. Like most other tadpoles, they have strong tails for swimming and rows of tiny "teeth."

Scientists changed the name of this species to *Rhinoderma rufum*. Clearly, it was closely related to Darwin's frogs. Because it is found only in Chile, it is commonly known as the Chile Darwin's frog. The Chilean common name for this frog is *sapito vaquero*, meaning "cowboy frog." The name refers to the frog's call, which reminds one of cowboys whistling to their cattle to speed them up.

Both species of frogs lived side by side near Concepción, Chile. Darwin's frog has a much larger geographical range, however. Chile Darwin's frog is known only from a small area in central Chile from sea level up to 500 meters (1,640 feet).

People have spent many hundreds of hours searching for Chile Darwin's frogs, even though they may be extinct. Not one has been found for the past three decades. Scientists still look for these frogs because they don't want to believe that this unique animal is gone. Much of the species' previous forest habitat has been destroyed and replaced with pine trees. Other areas have been converted to residential areas for humans.

Conservation Status

In 2010, the International Union for Conservation of Nature (IUCN) listed Darwin's frog, *Rhinoderma darwinii*, as "vulnerable." This designation means that the species is likely to become endangered unless the circumstances threatening its survival improve. Although the frogs are still locally common in some areas, populations are declining or disappearing in other areas, including protected parks and reserves.

Fundación Senda Darwin

Fundación Senda Darwin is a private nonprofit organization that supports ecological research and education. It is based at the biological station Senda Darwin—meaning "Darwin's Trail"—located in the northern part of Chiloé Island, in the south of Chile. Charles Darwin, the famous British naturalist and discoverer of Darwin's frogs, traveled on the old road winding through the property. The station was founded in 1995 as a base camp for scientists to carry out studies on the fauna and flora of Chilean rain forests, such as Darwin's frogs. Visiting Chilean and international scientists can stay in the residence house, use the laboratory facilities, and work in the surrounding forest. The station also provides opportunities for local landowners, students, teachers, children, and tourists to learn about the native forest ecosystems. Darwin's frogs live in the remnant forests around the station.

Glossary

absorb. To take in, especially through the movement of water and/or dissolved substances into cells, tissues, or organisms.

aquatic. Living in the water.

brooding male. In the case of Darwin's frogs, a male that is carrying tadpoles in his vocal sac.

cargo. Load that is carried, such as on a truck or ship, or in a male's vocal sac.

clutch. All the eggs laid at one time by a female frog.

descendant. Offspring of a certain ancestor; for example, you are your grandmother's descendant.

endangered. In danger of becoming extinct.

extinction. Dying out of a species.

flagging tape. Plastic tape used by scientists, foresters, and others to mark a spot so that it can be found again.

habitat. Natural place where an animal usually lives.

herpetologist. Scientist who studies amphibians and reptiles.

inflated. Swelled out, filled with air.

ingest. To take food into the body for digestion.

metamorphosis. Process of changing from the larval body form to the young-adult body form, as in from tadpole to froglet; an individual that has gone through metamorphosis is said to have metamorphosed.

nutrients. Molecules of food that living organisms take into their bodies; nutrients are used for growth, reproduction, and maintaining the body.

petiole. Stalk that connects a leaf blade to the stem.

predator. Animal that hunts other animals for food.

preserved specimen. Animal or plant that has been soaked in alcohol or formalin to keep it from rotting.

secretion. Substance released by a plant or animal.

site. Place or location.

species. All the individuals that could breed successfully with one another if they were in the same place, but not with individuals of other species.

terraria. Plural of terrarium.

terrarium. Enclosure for keeping small animals.

vocal sac. Throat pouch that fills with air when a male frog calls.

To Learn More

Books

Badger, David. *Frogs.* Stillwater, MN: Voyageur Press, 1995.

Clarke, Barry. *Amphibian.* Eyewitness Books. New York: DK Publishing, 2000.

Collard, Sneed B., III. *Animal Dads.* New York: Houghton Mifflin, 1997.

Crump, Marty. *Amphibians and Reptiles: An Introduction to Their Natural History and Conservation.* Granville, OH: McDonald & Woodward Publishing, 2011.

Kalman, Bobbie, and Tammy Everts. *Frogs and Toads.* New York: Crabtree Publishing, 1994.

Kalman, Bobbie, and Kathryn Smithyman. *The Life Cycle of a Frog.* New York: Crabtree Publishing, 2002.

Mara, William P. *The Fragile Frog.* Morton Grove, IL: Albert Whitman, 1996.

Miller, Sara Swan. *Amazing Amphibians.* New York: Franklin Watts, 2001.

Owen, Oliver S. *Tadpole to Frog.* Lifewatch: The Mystery of Nature. Edina, MN: Abdo & Daughters, 1994.

Pringle, Laurence. *Frogs! Strange and Wonderful.* Honesdale, PA: Boyds Mills Press, 2012.

Sill, Cathryn. *About Amphibians: A Guide for Children.* Atlanta, GA: Peachtree Publishers, 2000.

Souza, Dorothy M. *Frogs, Frogs Everywhere.* Minneapolis, MN: Carolrhoda Books, 1995.

Townsend, John. *Incredible Amphibians.* Mankato, MN: Heinemann-Raintree, 2005.

Turner, Pamela S. *The Frog Scientist.* New York: Houghton Mifflin Books for Children, 2009.

Wechsler, Doug. *Frog Heaven: Ecology of a Vernal Pool.* Honesdale, PA: Boyds Mills Press, 2006.

Williams, Brian. *Amazing Reptiles and Amphibians.* Pleasantville, NY: Gareth Stevens Publishing, 2008.

Websites*

The Basics about Frogs and Toads, with Lots of Links to Other Frog and Toad Websites

    42explore.com/frogs.htm

Frogland! A Wealth of Fun Information

    allaboutfrogs.org

Center for Global Environmental Education, Hamline University

    cgee.hamline.edu/frogs/science/frogfact.html

All about Frogs for Kids and Teachers

    kiddyhouse.com/Themes/frogs

Frog Activities, Facts, and Photos

    kidzone.ws/lw/frogs

Advancing the Conservation of Darwin's Frogs (A Project of the Atlanta Botanical Garden with the National Zoo of Chile)

    savedarwinsfrogs.org

Save the Frogs! America's First and Only Public Charity Dedicated to Amphibian Conservation

    savethefrogs.com

Bibliography

Burger, O. 1905. "La Neomelia de la *Rhinoderma darwinii* D. & B." *Memorias Científicas I Literarias* (Chile) 115: 585–604.

Busse, K. 1970. "Care of the Young by Male *Rhinoderma darwinii*." Copeia: 395.

Busse, K. 1989. "Zum Brutpflegeverhalten des Nasenfrosches *Rhinoderma darwinii* (Anura: Rhinodermatidae)." *Tier und Museum* 1 (3): 59–63.

Busse, K. 1991. "Bemerkungen zum Fortpflanzungsverhalten und zur Zucht von *Rhinoderma darwinii*." *Herpetofauna* 13 (71): 11–21.

Busse, K. 2003. "Fortpflanzungsbiologie von *Rhinoderma darwinii* (Anura: Rhinodermatidae) und die Stammesgeschichtliche und Funktionelle Verkettung der Einzelnen Verhaltensabläufe." *Bonner Zoologische Beiträge* 51: 3–34.

*Active at time of publication

Crump, M. L. 2002. "Natural History of Darwin's Frog, *Rhinoderma darwinii*." *Herpetological Natural History* 9 (1): 21–30.

Crump, M. L. 2003. "Vocal Sac-brooding Frogs (Rhinodermatidae)." In *Grzimek's Animal Life Encyclopedia*, 2nd ed., vol. 6, *Amphibians*, ed. M. Hutchins, W. E. Duellman, and N. Schlager (Farmington Hills, MI: Gale Group), 173–77.

Crump, M. L., and A. Veloso. 2005. "El Aporte de Observaciones de Terreno y del Análisis Genético para la Conservación de *Rhinoderma darwinii* en Chile." In *Historia, Biodiversidad y Ecología de los Bosques Costeros de Chile*, ed. C. Smith-Ramírez, J. J. Armesto, and C. Valdovinos (Santiago, Chile: Editorial Universitaria), 452–55.

Formas, R., E. Pugin, and B. Jorquera. 1975. "La Identidad del Batracio Chileno *Heminectes rufus* Philippi, 1902." *Physis* Sección C 34 (89): 147–57.

Goicoechea, O., O. Garrido, and B. Jorquera. 1986. "Evidence for a Trophic Paternal-larval Relationship in the Frog *Rhinoderma darwinii*." *Journal of Herpetology* 20 (2): 168–78.

Guichenot, A. 1848. "Reptilia et Pisces." In Gay, C. (Hrsg): *Historia Física y Política de Chile*; Zool.2, en casa del autor, Paris: 121-23.

Jiménez de la Espada, D. M. 1872. "Sobre la Reproducción de *Rhinoderma darwinii*." *Anales de la Sociedad Española de Historia Natural I*: 139–51

Jorquera, B. 1986. "Biología de la Reproducción del Género *Rhinoderma*." *Anales del Museo de Historia Natural de Valparaíso* 17: 53–62.

Jorquera, B., E. Pugin, O. Garrido, O. Goicoechea, and R.Formas. 1981. "Procedimiento de Desarrollo en Dos Especies del Género *Rhinoderma*." *Medio Ambiente* 5 (1–2): 58–71.

Werning, H. 2009. "From Darwin's Treasure Chest: *Rhinoderma*."*IRCF Reptiles & Amphibians* 16 (4): 246–55.

Wilhelm, O. 1927. "La *Rhinoderma darwinii* D. y B." *Boletin de la Sociedad de Biología de Concepción* (Chile) 1: 11–39.

Wilhelm, O. 1932. "Nuevas Observaciones acerca de la Neomelia de la *Rhinoderma darwinii*." *Revista Chilena de Historia Natural* 36: 166–70.

Author's Note

I first heard about Darwin's frogs forty-five years ago, as an undergraduate student at the University of Kansas. Never did I dream that one day I would study these frogs in their natural habitat. For many glorious days of working to add pieces to the Darwin's-frog puzzle, I thank my field companions in Chile: Andres Charrier, César Cuevas, Danté Fenolio, Antonieta Labra, William Lamar, Marco Méndez, Lauren Schneider, Eduardo Soto, Alberto Veloso, Eliseo Vergara, and Martín Zordan. Our research would not have been possible without the financial and logistical support of the National Geographic Society, the Atlanta Botanical Garden, and the National Zoo (Santiago, Chile). I thank Klaus Busse for sharing with me his vast knowledge of Darwin's frogs. Klaus, Andres, Danté, and Alan Savitzky generously allowed me to include their photographs and sketches. Finally, I thank Andy Boyles and Boyds Mills Press for believing in this book.

Dedication

For Fionna. May your life be filled with fanciful frogs. —*MC*

A portion of the proceeds from this book will be donated to the Fundación Senda Darwin.

Text copyright © 2013 by Marty Crump

Illustrations copyright © 2013 by Steve Jenkins and Edel Rodriguez

Image credits

Photographs: 2, 9 (top), 29, 31 (bottom): Danté Fenolio; 4, 7, 9 (bottom), 11 (bottom), 12, 19, 21, 23, 24, 25 (top), 27 (bottom), 31 (top), 32, 34, 35, 36, 38, 40: Marty Crump; 10-11 (top), 22, 26, 27 (top), 37: Andres Charrier; 15: Klaus Busse; 25 (bottom): Alan Savitzky.

Illustrations: 1, 5, 10-11, 13, 17, 28-29 (frogs): Steve Jenkins, after sketches by Klaus Busse; 6, 8, 10, 14, 28-29 (portraits): Edel Rodriguez; 6, 18, 28-29 (map, timeline, silhouettes): Ken Krug.

Boyds Mills Press, Inc.

815 Church Street

Honesdale, Pennsylvania 18431

Printed in China

ISBN: 978-1-59078-864-6

Library of Congress Control Number: 2012947844

First edition

10 9 8 7 6 5 4 3 2 1